Techniques for Sales Negotiation

Learn to Close Easily

Jeffrey Jasper

First published by Jefrey Jasper Copyright © 2024
All rights reserved. No part of this publication may be reproduced, stored or transmitted in any form or by any means, electronic, mechanical, photocopying, recording,scanning, or otherwise without written permission from the publisher. It is illegal to copy this book, post it to website, or distribute it by any other means without permission.

First edition 2024

Table of contents

Introduction — 7
   The Role of Negotiation in Modern Sales — 7
   The Evolution of Sales Negotiation Practices — 10
   The Art of Building Win-Win Scenarios — 15

Chapter 1 — 19
The Science of Negotiation — 19
   Understanding Negotiation Psychology — 19
   The key Traits of Successful Negotiators — 20
   How to Develop a Negotiator's Mindset — 23

Chapter 2 — 27
Preparation for Negotiation Success
   Researching Your Prospect — 27
   Setting Clear Goals and Defining Your Limits — 29
   Creating A Strong Value Proposition — 31

Chapter 3 — 33
Understanding Buyers Behavior — 33
   Identifying Buyer Personas — 33
   Recognizing Buying Signals — 36
   The Role of Emotions in Decision-Making — 39

Chapter 4 — 43
Effective Communication in Negotiation — 43
   The Power of Active Listening — 43
   Asking The Right Questions — 45
   Non-verbal Cues and Body Language — 50

Chapter 5 — 55
Strategies for Persuasion — 55
   Leveraging Scarcity and Urgency — 55
   Storytelling to Build Emotional Connections — 60
   Using Social Proof and Authority — 65

Chapter 6 — 69
Overcoming Objections — 69
   Identifying Common Objections — 69
   Techniques for Turning "No" to "Yes" — 71
   Maintaining control without being Overbearing — 74

Chapter 7 — 77
Collaboration Negotiation Strategies — 77
   Building Long-Term Relationships — 77
   Techniques for Creating Mutually Beneficial Outcomes — 80
   How to stay flexible without compromising Value — 85

Chapter 8 — 91
Navigating Complex Negotiations — 91
   Multiparty Negotiations — 91
   Dealing with Power Imbalances — 96
   Negotiating in High-stakes scenarios — 101

Chapter 9 — 107
Negotiating in a Digital Era — 107
- Virtual Negotiation Best Practices — 107
- Using Technology And Tools to Your Advantage — 112
- Managing Remote Buyer Interactions — 117

Chapter 10 — 123
Closing The Deal — 123
- Techniques for a Seamless Close — 123
- Recognizing the Right Time to Seal the Agreement — 127
- Handling Last-Minute Pushbacks — 129

Chapter 11 — 133
Evaluation Negotiation Outcomes — 133
- Measuring Success Beyond Numbers — 133
- Learning from Successes and Failures — 139
- Implementing Feedback for Future Growth — 142

Chapter 12 — 148
Maintaining The Relationship — 148
- Post Negotiation Follow-Up Strategies — 148
- Building Client Loyalty Through Trust and Value — 149
- Turning Clients into Advocates — 153

CONCLUSION — 154

Power of Negotiation

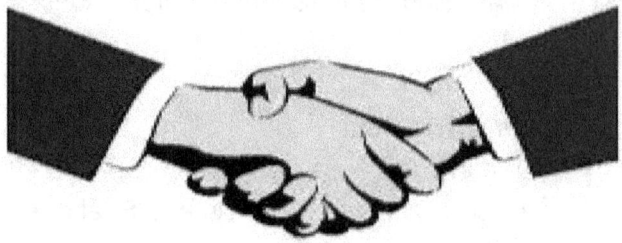

There is power in creative negotiation. And, if properly applied, could be the key that helps you get more performance contracts. One must know the secrets of constructive negotiation and how to make it work for you.

Introduction

The Role of Negotiation in Modern Sales

Sarah sat across from Tom, her face furrowed in a scowl. They were so close to completing the agreement! "I just don't get it," she moaned. What took place?

Tom took a deep breath and sat back in his chair. Sarah, it's the same old tale. We must improve our negotiating skills. We must realize that the product is no longer the only consideration. It's about establishing connections and identifying points of agreement.

Sarah's eyebrows went up. However, we've always been adept at fostering connections. What has changed?

Tom laughed. "Sarah, the game has changed. It's not a one-way street anymore. Customers are more demanding, knowledgeable, and likely to leave if unappreciated. We must change or risk falling behind.

Sarah gave a contemplative nod. "So, what do you think we need to do differently?"

Tom grinned. "The skill of bargaining must be our main priority. We must develop our ability to actively listen, pose perceptive queries, and come up with original ideas that work for everyone. We must be able to decipher nonverbal cues and predict customer demands.

Sarah's gaze brightened. "That's a terrific concept! However, how can we acquire that skill?
After some time, Tom said, "We start by reading." We attend courses, study negotiating books, and speak with seasoned salesmen. We gain knowledge from their errors and achievements. Above all else, we practice. With each client, we practice daily until it comes naturally to us.
Sarah grinned. "I'm on board. Let's get this done.
Tom grinned back. "All right. because it is essential to the future of sales.

The changing role of bargaining in contemporary sales is discussed in the conversation between Sarah and Tom. The first real-world example is a lost sales opportunity.

The reader is instantly drawn in by this realistic scenario and is prompted to think about the fundamental causes of the deal's failure.
The more seasoned salesman, Tom, determines that the problem stems from a lack of skillful bargaining. He highlights that creating win-win solutions and fostering strong connections are much more important in modern sales than just focusing on the product or service.

The discussion then dives into the three essential components of a successful negotiation: creative problem-solving, perceptive questioning, and active listening. Tom emphasizes how crucial it is to adjust to the evolving demands and expectations of customers.
The final recommendation is to study, practice, and become an expert negotiator.
Salespeople may position themselves for future success and close more transactions by doing this.

The Evolution of Sales Negotiation Practices

When you reach the negotiation stage of the selling process, you could lose the sale in an instant, regardless of how long you spend working on it—nine hours, nine weeks, or nine months. Furthermore, the sellers who win the sale may not benefit the most from the negotiated outcome.. In negotiations, some sellers lose the majority of their margin even though they make sales. At the last minute, final agreements are frequently subject to budgetary constraints or changes.

It makes sense why a lot of sellers are nervous about negotiations. Anxiety is actually the most prevalent emotion linked to negotiations, according to numerous studies, and our fieldwork demonstrates that nervous negotiators perform poorly.

Negotiation is more complicated now than it was even ten years ago because procurement is more involved, which makes matters even more difficult.

All kinds of buyers are better informed about you, your products, your rivals, and your costs.

Third parties frequently act as a mediator between buyers and sellers, protecting the former from the latter.

Technologies for procurement are quickly taking over.

Because of this, you, the seller, may believe that the buyer has all the power. Not at all.

Indeed, an article about negotiations in the Harvard Business Review begins, "The balance of power has dramatically shifted from buyers to suppliers in many industries."

Most of the time, a sales negotiation is crucial to the buyer and seller's success or failure.

Negotiating the best deals requires skill on the part of both buyers and sellers. They must know how to react to the other party no matter what is thrown at them and employ the best sales negotiation techniques, approaches, and tactics when needed.

Do you want to learn how to sell much more than you currently do as a salesperson?

If you don't learn how to sell more, you might be among the people who are far below average, and you know that you're going to lose your job. An average salesperson might think, "Hey, I need to get really good at this so I can control my own destiny, make more sales, and make more money." Even though you're a good salesperson, you may be thinking, "Man, I want to become the best in my office, the number one person, get all the company awards." Alternatively, you may be the best in your company but believe that you need to learn more in order to become the best in the entire industry, where everyone knows that you are the best, no question about that.

I'm going to show you what is referred to as the "new model of selling" by tens of thousands of salespeople in almost every country and industry if you're an entrepreneur, business owner, salesperson, sales manager, coach, consultant, or anybody else who sells anything and wants to convince anyone to do anything.

I'm going to dissect the new selling model in contrast to the one where you may have been pressured to sell by your employer or a sales guru who hasn't sold in decades or has never been a very successful salesperson. I'll explain the new selling model to you and provide several examples that are specific to your industry as I move over to the vibe board. Come on over here, and I'll show you how to increase sales of your goods or services.

Okay, now I'll demonstrate the distinctions between the so-called old and new models of selling. After that, I'll give you some examples from the industry and sort of explain the psychology of each NEPQ stage.

The acronym for this question is **NEPQ**, is Neuro-Emotional Persuasion Question. This is the **AIDA** model of selling, which is somewhat similar to the traditional approach. You may have heard of consultative selling, which is another name for it. This is known as more of the older model, the AIDA system. Additionally, it is reframed as consultative selling. It represents Attention, interest, desire, and action.

Let me briefly discuss this in comparison to NEPQ, which we refer to as the new selling model—Neuro-Emotional Persuasion Questions. Old model, new model. Now, if you pay close attention, some of you may recognize this.

I will simply explain this to you. The first 10% was the previous model, and I was genuinely attempting to establish a rapport. Sayings like "Hey, how are you today?" became second nature to you. How are you today? What's the weather like? Where do you live if you use Zoom? Do you have a phone call? Did you watch the game last night?

You were attempting to connect with shared values—that's the way you were taught to establish rapport, isn't it? Since your prospects have heard that before, we refer to it as "fake rapport." Which questions are they accustomed to asking? "How are you today?" is a question that every salesperson who has ever attempted to sell them anything asks. How are you finding the day? How is the climate there? Many prospects interpret those kinds of questions because they are aware of your goals.

The Art of Building Win-Win Scenarios

Win-win negotiations are those in which both the buyer and the seller are satisfied with the outcome. Instead of emphasizing immediate rewards, this cooperative strategy aims to create lasting partnerships.

A win-win scenario exists in sales negotiations. There are situations where you desire a certain conclusion, but you also want the other person to win, so both parties benefit. This is known as a win-win situation. Of course, there are certain things you have to compromise on and find a middle ground on, but you're fighting for the person you're negotiating with, the client you're trying to sell to, or, you know, whoever is on the other side. It's a win-win scenario where both parties are putting their lips together, so it's not very selfish.

Win-lose situations are extremely self-centered, with one side showing little concern for the other, and you're thinking, "You know what?" Because I want this, I'm going to make things tough, so the other person won't be happy; they won't work with your heart and soul, and you will burn through. Imagine you saying "I don't care about you right now". You might win once, but you will lose a relationship.

The third is a lose-win situation where we believe that everyone is here to cheat us or let us give up, and you simply can't fight and give in easily. You're not the negotiating type, which is very hurtful because it means you won't be in business for very long and you'll eventually lose; you'll be depressed, but even if you do end up getting a job there, you'll be taken advantage of.

I will return to win-win, and the reason it is crucial is because in a win-win situation, you truly need to develop innovative ways and means to find out what the other person wants. What do you want? and how both parties stand to gain, correct? Not in a sales setting! If someone is in need of entertainment and you are a TV salesman, you might tell them, "Look, my TV will get you Bluetooth this and a smart display, and you can connect with an HDMI and blah blah blah!.

That way you get the best kind of entertainment, and by the way, I'll also give you a little discount." In other words, you are selling a TV to someone who needs one by highlighting features that may persuade them to buy it. You're not attempting to just tell someone, "Hey, you don't need this, but just take it because I could sell it and meet my sales goals, and I don't care about you; I only care about myself." That's a poor scenario to be in, and most of the time, people will be dismissive of you.

In order to clinch a transaction with a win-win situation, it is vital to pinpoint the prospect's pain spots and describe the product's amazing features. This will make the prospect fall in love with the product and enable them to purchase it at the same time.

Chapter 1

The Science of Negotiation

Understanding Negotiation Psychology

The complex relationship between psychological variables and negotiation dynamics is explored in negotiation psychology. During negotiations, it examines how social interactions, emotions, perceptions, and biases influence communication and decision-making. Having a better knowledge of these psychological factors may help negotiators establish rapport, communicate more effectively, and reach win-win agreements. Numerous psychological ideas are examined in this field of study, such as anchoring, framing effects, social proof, and cognitive biases, in order to shed light on how negotiators can successfully negotiate complex situations, influence others, and ultimately come to agreements that meet the needs of all parties.

Negotiations are a psychological dance that involves more than just numbers. By using techniques like mirroring body language, asking open-ended questions, and demonstrating empathy, you can establish rapport and trust. By comprehending your counterpart's needs and matching them with your own, you can create a win-win situation. These small psychological gimmicks can turn negotiations from a conflict into a cooperative endeavor that builds relationships and produces positive results. Make use of psychology in negotiations to transform possible disputes into opportunities.

The key Traits of Successful Negotiators

Having trouble achieving your goals in negotiations? I'm sharing three essential traits that distinguish successful negotiators from others, and this could transform your approach forever! Achieving success in negotiation involves more than just mastering tactics; it requires the mindset to overcome obstacles.

Let's explore how determination, resilience, and self-confidence can significantly enhance your negotiation results.

Unyielding determination is the motivation that drives you toward your objectives, regardless of how tough the journey becomes. It entails staying dedicated and focused, even when you encounter setbacks. Determined negotiators persist; they adjust and discover alternative routes to reach their goals. Consider how Michael Jordan or Kobe Bryant had to adapt in the peak moments of the playoffs to secure their victories. You should keep progressing and understand that every obstacle presents a chance to fine-tune your approach. Thus, remain determined and allow your passion to propel you onward. Resilience refers to your capacity to recover from setbacks and continue your journey.

In negotiations, challenges are unavoidable, but resilient negotiators interpret them as temporary obstacles rather than permanent impediments. They uphold an optimistic perspective and adapt to tough situations. By cultivating resilience, you can navigate difficulties and emerge even more capable. Always remember, every setback sets the stage for a comeback. Having self-belief is vital.

This confidence enables you to stand your ground, even when met with opposition or doubt. Reflect on Martin Luther King Jr.; his self-belief empowered him to chase his dream. Consider any world leader, business executive, or athlete; all require self-confidence to attain greatness. Self-belief also involves adhering to your core values and not compromising them for convenience. Throughout negotiations, you will inevitably encounter doubt or disapproval from others. Successful negotiators harness dissent as a source of strength and motivation.

Being doubted or disapproved of, can serve as a potent catalyst, propelling you toward exceptional results. View all the critics and naysayers as a source of fuel. Use this energy to inspire you. Think of the most talented artists; if you're a hip-hop fan, consider 50 Cent or Eminem. They use that negative energy to drive them in creating superior albums, music, and products. This mindset will empower you to pursue your goals with increased determination.

Being resilient against criticism and failure is crucial. Criticism and failure are natural components of any negotiation, but with steadfast confidence, you can perceive criticism as constructive input and failure as a meaningful lesson. By embracing setbacks, you can constantly improve and remain committed to achieving success in negotiation. Your mindset is your greatest asset. Always remember to stay determined, be resilient, and maintain faith in your abilities. Together, let's dominate the negotiation table!

How to Develop a Negotiator's Mindset

My negotiation cap is the first thing I grab and head out the door when my father calls me to go shopping. He's a lawyer by trade, so it's not that he can't. His preference is to avoid doing so unless it is absolutely required. I therefore seize the chance to improve and refine my negotiating abilities, whereas others shudder at the idea of having to haggle. I follow my mother's mantra: Closed mouths don't get fed.

"Ask for what you want or deserve, Jeff," she would say. "Unless you ask, you'll never know the answer. You may be pleasantly surprised by the answer you receive."

Throughout my career, I have adhered to and utilized this for things that I want and desire, such as a promotion at work or, in the case of my father, a discount on a new car at the Hyundai Distribution Center. But for me, developing my negotiating skills requires a lot of deliberate practice and is a continuous process.

For anyone, negotiating can be a difficult undertaking. If I told you that you negotiate every day, you probably wouldn't believe me. However, we feel a little vulnerable when we have to bargain for something that has a lot on the line; we don't want to ask for the wrong thing in the wrong way. Of course, when you are negotiating with someone in a position of authority, such as your boss, an investor, or a possible business partner, these feelings of vulnerability are heightened. But if you are prepared and have the correct attitude, you will have the courage to ask that daring question. However, what is the process?

Create the Correct Attitude

Maintaining composure and self-assurance is the first step in cultivating the proper mindset. It's critical to keep your emotions under control during the entire negotiating process. To replicate the role of the counterpart, try practicing with someone you are at ease with and who can push back. Writing notes in advance, in my opinion, helps you stay focused and keep things in perspective. These actions will help you cultivate a positive outlook, boost your self-esteem beforehand, and keep emotional control.

Make an agenda

Creating your agenda is one of the most important aspects of negotiating. Be clear about what you hope to gain from the negotiation and what you will have to give up in order to get there. Once more, when the time comes to ask, it might be useful to write these things down. Furthermore, being aware of your bottom line—the lowest sum of money or other factors that will make a deal acceptable—will help you avoid making needless compromises.

Be well-prepared

Have a purpose when you negotiate. It will be difficult to determine whether the proposal is good or bad if you don't know exactly what you're negotiating for. Your ability to make an informed choice will improve with the amount of information and knowledge you possess.

Before engaging in a negotiation, learn as much as you can about the subject, including its advantages and disadvantages as well as the opinions of others. How has this matter been addressed previously? What options do you have on this subject? Who else could be affected by your decision, and what would they think? If things don't go according to plan, who wins?

This information-gathering procedure can assist in identifying the issues that are most crucial to both parties and in figuring out who has the most influence over whom.

Chapter 2

Preparation for Negotiation Success

Researching Your Prospect

Research indicates that more than 40% of sales representatives find prospecting challenging — the act of identifying and connecting with potential clients. Prior to initiating contact, it's crucial to familiarize yourself with the client in order to determine if pursuing them aligns with your business goals.

Having relevant background information can significantly influence a business relationship, yet this remains a common challenge for many salespeople. So, what steps can you take to investigate prospects before a call or meeting to ensure that the interaction is beneficial for both parties? This book will outline the essential steps to gain a solid understanding of your prospect using available resources while effectively managing your time.

Understanding the significance of researching your sales leads is essential. A sales lead is an individual who is aware of your product or service but has not yet engaged with you or your organization. To guide them into the sales funnel, you need to comprehend their position, business interests, industry, and challenges. This information will enable you to engage with them in a manner that highlights the value you can provide. Ineffective client engagement often stems from insufficient information. Before you make that phone call or enter the meeting, you should have a comprehensive understanding of your client.

When discussing a sale with your prospect, it should not feel like you are contacting an entirely unfamiliar person. By that stage, they should already feel like someone you know well. This thorough understanding of prospects is one of the essential proactive sales strategies to enhance the likelihood of success.

Setting Clear Goals and Defining Your Limits

The finer points and intricacies of this process should be examined when setting your negotiation goals in the area of auction negotiation skills. Here are some crucial things to remember:

1. **Make sure your goals are clear**: It's important to know exactly what you want to achieve before you enter into any negotiations. Do you want a win-win solution, the biggest profit, or the lowest cost? Setting clear objectives will help you stay on course during the negotiation.

2. **Sort your interests by importance:** Set aside time to identify your top priorities. This will ensure that you focus on what really matters to you and help you make informed decisions during the negotiation.

3. **Research and gather data**: Information is essential in negotiations. Investigate the auction, the product or service being offered, and the other bidders in great detail. You will be better equipped to make wise decisions and bargain from a position of strength as a result.

4. **Respect differing points of view**: It's critical to consider the opinions of each party involved in the negotiation. Through understanding their needs, constraints, and motivations, you can find common ground and investigate win-win solutions.

5. **Use your communication skills:** In order to negotiate successfully, you must communicate well. To ensure mutual understanding, state your goals clearly, listen intently to the other person, and ask clarifying questions. A positive and cooperative negotiating environment will result from this.

6. **Use examples to elucidate concepts**: It can be helpful to include examples that highlight key points and demonstrate the ideas being discussed. These

kinds of examples can help the reader understand the material and make it more relatable.

Creating A Strong Value Proposition

Value proposition is a concise statement that clarifies why a consumer should select your product or service. It showcases the unique advantages and value of your offering, setting it apart from competitors while addressing customer needs. An effective value proposition focuses on how your product or service enhances the customer's experience or resolves their issues from their perspective. It is crucial for generating interest, fostering trust, and increasing both new and repeat customers.

- **Understand your customer**: Recognize their aspirations, needs, and challenges.
- **Highlight unique advantages:** What distinguishes your offering?

- **Emphasize the solutions:** Clearly show how your product or service addresses problems.
- **Keep it straightforward and clear**: Refrain from using technical jargon or complex language.
- **Assess the value:** Provide data that illustrates the effect of your offering.
- **Test and refine**: Gather feedback to enhance your proposal.
- **Use an engaging format**: A clear and concise message is vital.

Chapter 3

Understanding Buyers Behavior

Identifying Buyer Personas

Buyer personas are essential to your marketing strategy. The ideal representation of a potential customer is portrayed by these fictional characters. The advantage of developing personas is that the insights gained can lead to informed choices about how to effectively connect with and engage your target audience, enabling you to attract and win over customers successfully.

Priorities obviously change as consumers move from buying a product to using it. Because of this, a lot of businesses create two different kinds of personas: buyer and user. Knowing what matters most at different stages of the customer journey helps your business provide a Comprehensive

Product Experience, even if the people these persodrivesnas represent are the same.

What the creation of buyer personas by marketing teams?

Buyer personas help you understand the "why" behind your marketing decisions and serve as a guide for all aspects of marketing. You can improve your relationship with your customers by learning more about their demographics, behavioral patterns, goals, and motivations. When developing your marketing strategies, this research should be a key component that guides how you communicate about your product and reach specific customer segments.

Some major advantages of creating buyer personas::
Know who your ideal clients are and what matters to them.

Create messaging and positioning that genuinely connects.

Concentrate on tasks, campaigns, and programs that have an impact.

Improve the buyer journey to cultivate and attract more clients.

Buyer personas are commonly created by product marketing to help shape the company's go-to-market strategy for a product or service. Other members of the marketing team can then use these buyer personas to direct their work, from creating content to improving acquisition funnels. Additionally, buyer personas are useful tools for teaching the sales force how to recognize your ideal target market.

Recognizing Buying Signals

What is the best method for accelerating an uncertain buyer's journey?

More than just hot takes and tips and tricks will be required. The foundation of a truly effective GTM motion is the large-scale conversion of signals into action.

Purchasing Signals: What Are They?

Data points known as buying signals indicate when a target customer might be ready to buy your goods or services. When used appropriately, these signals which can originate from a wide range of sources and take many different forms, can streamline the infamously complex B2B sales cycle.

Benefits of Buying Signals

Determine the main trends and activities among your client.

Lead you to potential customers when they're most likely to pay attention.

Emphasize updates that keep you informed about current accounts.

Customize suggestions for more individualized interactions with clients and potential customers.

Sales and marketing teams can better target their efforts to the needs of their customers by familiarizing themselves with the various buying signals found in this data trail.

What Makes Buying Signals Crucial?
Knowing and utilizing buying signals changes the way you interact with both present and future clients. By paying attention to these indicators, you create the conditions for a more intelligent and considerably more successful approach.

By indicating the customer's present position in the sales funnel, buying signals provide a distinctive window into their journey. Reacting to buying signals guarantees that your message is received when it counts most, whether that be through the timing of a follow-up call or the personalization of marketing collateral.
Recognizing and responding to these signals can make the difference between a deal being closed

and an opportunity being lost in the intricate world of business-to-business sales.

How to Implement Buying Signals
Buying signals can be used at any point in the customer lifecycle.
Sales and marketing teams can execute more coordinated actions that yield tangible outcomes by methodically monitoring and reacting to signals.
While the sales team contacts customers via phone, email, or social media messaging, the marketing team can use signals to guide marketing automation and social and display .
Even cold leads can be reactivated by using buying signals.
You can spot rekindled interest and modify your strategy to successfully re-engage them by keeping an eye on their recent activity.

Existing customers can also benefit from signals. You can stay ahead of any potential dissatisfaction with your product offering or services and identify upsell opportunities by keeping track of the signals that appear for your current clients.

In summary, buying signals help increase sales. You put yourself in a position to offer highly targeted, individualized sales and marketing at the appropriate moment when you pay attention to the signals from your customers and prospects.

It's simpler to grab your prospect's attention, anticipate their problems, reduce their resistance, and, of course, close the deal if you use the appropriate signals at the right moment.

Create your signal-based sales motion now to begin closing deals more quickly and with less work.

The Role of Emotions in Decision-Making

The act of negotiating is fundamentally human. It's about people, each of whom brings their own viewpoints, aspirations, and feelings to the table; it's not just about numbers, terms, and conditions. Early in my career, I frequently undervalued the importance of emotions in negotiations in favor of the deal's more concrete features.

However, I learned from the experience that the human element is a driving force that shapes the negotiation landscape rather than being a peripheral factor.

The Emotional Dance

Emotions guide the steps in negotiations, which are like a dance. Imagine that you and HR are negotiating your pay, going over figures, benefits, and duties. Even though it might appear to be a simple conversation, there is a delicate emotional interplay going on underneath. The skill is in identifying these feelings and skillfully handling them.

Emotions in the context of negotiation can range from anticipation and excitement to anxiety and, occasionally, frustration. The way we interpret and react to these feelings can have a big impact on the negotiation process. Empathy is our most graceful partner in this dance, which enables us to navigate the emotional highs and lows of the negotiating process with ease.

Recognizing the Unspoken Problem

Let's talk about the fear of asking for what we want, which is the elephant in the negotiation room. There is frequently an undercurrent of trepidation when negotiating terms with a client, a business deal, or a salary. I can speak from experience when I say that our ability to negotiate can be hampered by our fear of rejection or of coming across as overly assertive.

Navigating the emotional terrain of negotiation begins with understanding and admitting these fears. After all, negotiating is a high-stakes situation, so it's acceptable to feel anxious or apprehensive. Understanding these feelings enables us to negotiate authentically, opening the door to a more candid and open discussion.

The Influence of Compassion in Bargaining.

The unsung hero of negotiating techniques is empathy. It entails genuinely placing ourselves in other people's shoes in addition to comprehending their feelings. For instance, empathy enables us to understand the other party's viewpoint during salary negotiations with HR, including their priorities, limitations, and goals.

I've learned from my own negotiation experience that empathy is a strength rather than a weakness. It's the capacity to establish a rapport and cultivate an atmosphere in which both sides feel heard and understood. Empathy turns a negotiation from a combative conflict into a cooperative discussion in which understanding between the parties serves as the link to a fruitful conclusion.

Negotiation is a shared journey toward a common goal, not a battleground. Negotiation is elevated from a transactional exchange to a transformative dialogue when we acknowledge the emotional currents at work. Without empathy, which enables us to navigate the complexities of human emotions with grace, the art of negotiation,whether it be regarding compensation, project terms, or business deals,is incomplete.

Therefore, keep this in mind the next time you're at the negotiating table: empathy is a strategy, not a compromise. The strategic advantage is what turns a negotiation into a fruitful and cooperative endeavor.

Chapter 4

Effective Communication in Negotiation

The Power of Active Listening

In the realm of marketing and sales negotiations, employing active listening brings numerous benefits. It aids in establishing rapport, building credibility, and fostering trust with clients and potential customers. Moreover, it allows you to gain a deeper understanding of their issues, concerns, and requirements, enabling you to tailor your solutions to meet their unique needs.

Active listening can also uncover opportunities for upselling and cross-selling as you gain insights into the client's business and the challenges they encounter. It further assists in effectively managing objections by allowing you to address concerns before they escalate into deal-breakers.

Suggestions for Enhancing Active Listening Skills During Sales and Marketing Negotiations

To enhance your active listening skills in sales and marketing discussions, consider these methods and strategies:

1. **Focus on the speaker**: Maintain eye contact and pay close attention to the individual speaking. Set aside your computer and phone to avoid distractions, and refrain from interrupting the speaker.
2. **Use open-ended questions**: Encourage the speaker to share more information by asking open-ended questions. For example, "Could you elaborate on that?" or "What led to that decision?"
3. **Rephrase and summarize**: This not only shows your active engagement in the conversation but also ensures that you have accurately understood the speaker's message.
4. **Acknowledge emotions:** Show your empathy and understanding towards the speaker's feelings. For example, "I understand why that would be upsetting for you."

Asking The Right Questions

Like master keys, good questions can open up a world of possibilities and unlock numerous doors, both personally and professionally. It's astonishing how many harmful and prevalent myths about them still exist, especially considering how crucial and effective they are to negotiation.

This might be due to the fact that "question asking" is not taught as a skill outside of professions like journalism, law, and medicine that particularly call for it.

Even worse, the importance of asking good questions is frequently completely ignored in the lessons we learn about how to approach negotiations. Both explicitly and implicitly, we are taught that we must promote ourselves, prove our worth, and sell ourselves. Instead of asking about the needs, wants, or desires of the other party, the path to success is to outline our demands and demonstrate our worth.

Furthermore, we've been taught to value and respect those who "play hardball." Thoughtful questioners and attentive listeners are often left in the background as dominant negotiators take center stage. As a result, a lot of people go into a negotiation believing that making their case and arguing for it should come first.

The fact is that showing interest in others by asking them questions and allowing them to speak makes it much easier to win their approval and support. This truth was expressed by Dale Carnegie almost a century ago in his seminal work on "How to Win Friends and Influence People" and numerous notable intellectuals have since repeated it. Nevertheless, a large number of us continue to fail to apply this crucial idea.

The good news is that anyone can learn this skill, and there is a limitless amount of room for improvement.

How can we start posing more insightful queries, then? First, let's think about why this is challenging in the first place.

Why it's hard to ask effective questions

This relates to yet another widely held belief that isn't always accurate: that negotiations are essentially hostile.

Questions will inevitably arise when one or both parties treat a negotiation as a zero-sum game, where your gain is my loss and vice versa. The other party's questions can make you feel vulnerable and suspicious, leading you to wonder, "Is this person trying to expose or exploit me?"

It is necessary to change the perspective from one of a competition for resources, with a definite winner and loser, to one of an opportunity to investigate new possibilities and value that result from teamwork in order to get around this aversion to questioning. And it's not always simple to stop thinking like this.

We'll discuss how to manage competitive versus collaborative conversations in more detail later in the piece, but first, let's examine the significance of good questioning.

The significance of asking good questions. Thinking about what occurs when you don't ask good questions is one way to answer this question. To put it briefly, a great deal of potential value is lost.

Asking the right questions can reveal a lot of important information and open doors that are advantageous to both sides. It's arguably one of the most dependable methods for reaching the desired "win-win" result that is frequently discussed during negotiations but is so infrequently realized. Going on the defensive is a common tactic used by negotiators, and if they are successful in asking questions, they usually do so in a way that, at best, does not elicit helpful information and, at worst, offends the other party.

This leads us to the second important advantage of asking good questions: it makes people feel more comfortable, strengthens relationships, and calms the room. People are far more likely to divulge information that could be helpful in a negotiation when they lower their guard. At any rate, you have more information at your disposal than if they hide away.

It's also crucial to remember that numerous studies have shown that the majority of people are unaware of the connection between positive regard and questioning. They might be able to recall being questioned during a conversation, but they usually aren't aware of how much of this contributes to the increased friendliness.

Therefore, asking good questions not only helps you get the information you need and want, but it also does so without drawing suspicion or raising red flags.

Furthermore, as we are all aware, friendly negotiations typically result in better outcomes than hostile ones.

Effective questioning is obviously underutilized, despite the fact that it can have incalculable advantages when executed properly.

Non-verbal Cues and Body Language

Understanding the nuances of body language can give you a big advantage at the negotiating table because it communicates your intentions, confidence, and emotions—all of which are crucial in determining how a negotiation turns out. We'll look at how to use body language to your advantage as a negotiator in this book. One keeps in close contact. A key component of effective body language in negotiations is ;

Maintaining good eye contact
Looking at someone in the eye communicates confidence and sincerity and shows that you are paying attention to the conversation. However, don't stare too much at once as this can come across as intimidating. Strive for friendly, natural eye contact.

Regulate your facial expressions

During negotiations, your face is a potent tool for expressing emotions. Controlling your facial expressions is crucial to preventing an overly large smile. Sincerely, when it's appropriate, take care not to unintentionally frown or smirk. Maintain neutral facial expressions or ones that reflect the negotiation's tone.

Keep your posture open

Your posture conveys a lot about your self-assurance and openness. Keep your body relaxed and open. One useful negotiating strategy is mirroring and matching your counterpart's body language, then abruptly mimicking their gestures, tone, and speech rate to build rapport and connect. Avoid crossing your arms, as this can convey defensiveness or resistance. Instead, sit or stand with your arms at your sides or use open gestures to show that you're open to the conversation. This strategy can promote trust and make negotiations go more smoothly.

Make hand gestures carefully

Hand gestures when negotiating, can be very effective, but they should be used carefully. Use your hands to highlight important points or to support your arguments. Steer clear of overly dramatic or distracting gestures as they can take attention away from your message.

Keep an eye on your voice and breathing because these can give away your emotional state. Confidence and control are communicated through deep, steady breathing and a cool, collected voice. Don't talk too softly or too quickly. Because this may indicate anxiety or a lack of confidence,

Control your anxious tendencies

Many people have nervous behaviors, such as fidgeting, playing with their hair, or tapping their fingers. Recognize and manage these behaviors as they can damage your credibility during a negotiation. concentrate on keeping a calm and still attitude throughout the exercises.

Listening actively

A crucial component of successful negotiation is active listening. Show that you are paying attention and being involved in the conversation by using nonverbal clues like nodding and keeping eye contact. This will encourage your counterpart to open up and share more details.

Keep emotional restraint

Negotiations may turn emotional. The negotiation process can be hampered by outbursts of rage or frustration, so it's imperative to keep emotional control. Use your body language to convey professionalism and poise.

While these guidelines are generally effective, nobody is willing to break the mold. Keep in mind that every negotiation is different, and there may be times when departing from these guidelines is required to accomplish your goals. Adjust your nonverbal cues to the unique circumstances of each negotiation outcome.

By deliberately controlling your non-verbal communication, you can gain a substantial advantage in accomplishing your objectives by becoming proficient in body language and negotiation. You can establish rapport, foster trust, and sway the outcome of negotiations to your advantage. Regularly using these strategies will make you a more skilled and assured negotiator over time.

Chapter 5

Strategies for Persuasion

Leveraging Scarcity and Urgency

Urgency and scarcity are strong psychological cues that have a big impact on consumer behavior and decision-making. While urgency generates a sense of immediate need or action, scarcity is the belief that a good, service, or opportunity is in limited supply. In persuasion, combining these two tactics can be very successful.

Leveraging scarcity allows you to capitalize on people's **FOMO** (fear of missing out). People may act quickly to protect something they believe to be scarce or running low due to this innate fear. Countdown timers on e-commerce websites, exclusive products, and limited-time offers are a few instances of scarcity in action.

Contrarily, urgency capitalizes on the need for instant satisfaction and the desire to avoid waiting. It encourages people to take immediate action in order to prevent the negative effects of missing out. Flash sales, time-sensitive discounts, and limited-quantity alerts are some strategies for generating urgency.

A careful balance must be struck when integrating these tactics into your persuasive efforts. Subtle and strategically placed applications can increase the perceived value of your offer, while overuse can breed suspicion and mistrust. For example, you can emphasize that only a few items are left in stock or that your special offer is about to expire in order to create a sense of urgency. When combined with real-time updates, like displaying the number of items sold or the amount of time left before the offer expires, this tactic can be especially successful.

Your persuasive efforts can also be strengthened by using urgency and personalized scarcity. A stronger sense of urgency can be produced by customizing messages for each customer based on their browsing history, preferences, or previous purchases. Sending them customized emails or alerts about special deals on products they've expressed interest in, for instance, can encourage quick action.

Using Stories to Create Emotional Bonds
One of the best strategies to establish an emotional bond with your audience is through storytelling. Stories arouse emotions, foster empathy, and help people remember information, which is why humans are naturally drawn to them. Storytelling can increase the relatability and persuasiveness of your message when used in persuasion.
Crafting a narrative that speaks to the values, experiences, and goals of your audience is essential to effective storytelling. Setting the scene at the beginning, presenting the conflict or challenge in the middle, and offering insight and resolution at the end are all essential components of a well-written story.

Pay attention to the following components to increase the persuasiveness of your story:

Character Development

Present likable, fully realized characters that your readers can relate to. Your target audience's experiences should be reflected in these characters' unique personalities, drives, and difficulties. Your audience will find it easier to identify with your message and see themselves in the story if you create characters that they can relate to.

As an example, emotional hooks To evoke strong emotions in your audience, use scenarios and language that are emotionally charged. Dramatic events, intimate tales, or poignant moments that evoke strong emotions can all serve as emotional hooks. Using these feelings—whether they be inspiration, fear, joy, or sadness—will help your story become more powerful and memorable.

Authenticity

When telling your story, be sincere and honest. Credibility and trust are increased by authenticity. Provide personal stories, endorsements, and real-world examples that highlight the benefits of your offering. Real stories have a higher chance of connecting with your audience and forging enduring bonds.

Visuals and Sensory Details

To make the experience more immersive, include sensory details and vivid descriptions. Your audience will be able to see, hear, smell, taste, and feel the elements of your story as you use words to paint a picture. Your audience will be drawn into the story by this sensory-rich storytelling, which will increase its persuasiveness and level of engagement.

Stories can be told in a variety of ways in the digital age, including podcasts, social media posts, videos, and written content. The secret is to use stories to support your arguments, emphasize advantages, and show how your offering can improve the lives of your target audience. To improve your storytelling and produce a more engaging experience, think about incorporating multimedia components like pictures, videos, and interactive content.

Storytelling to Build Emotional Connections

Logic, strategy, and persuasion are frequently used as lenses through which to view negotiation. Even though these components are obviously essential, storytelling is another potent instrument that can significantly increase a negotiation's efficacy. By emotionally connecting with opponents and making difficult ideas more relatable and memorable, good storytelling can help frame arguments, evoke empathy, and persuade them.

Using Stories to Frame Arguments

Storytelling is fundamentally about presenting facts in an engaging and understandable manner. Being able to tell a story while presenting your points can be very effective in negotiations. A well-written story can vividly and relatably illustrate the advantages of your proposal rather than delivering a dry argument or a list of facts. Instead of just saying that your product is more efficient, for instance, you could share a story about a client who had major problems and how your product revolutionized their operations, resulting in significant improvements. This strategy not only grabs attention but also increases the impact and memorability of your argument.

Creating Empathy via Similar Experiences

In negotiations, empathy is essential. Opponents are more likely to be receptive to your suggestions when they can see things from your point of view. Stories enable people to put themselves in other people's shoes, which makes them effective tools for generating empathy. You can humanize your arguments and make the other side feel more sympathetic to your point of view by providing personal tales or client success stories. A story about an employee's hardships and how better working conditions have improved their life, for example, you can make a stronger argument than just statistics when negotiating for better working

Know Your Audience

Craft a narrative that speaks to the other party's interests and worries. You can create a story that directly addresses their needs by taking the time to understand their point of view. This calls for careful planning and learning about the other party's needs. Examine their history, driving forces, and areas of discomfort. You can better align your story with their goals by knowing what motivates them and what they want to get out of the negotiation. Learn about the objectives, difficulties, and recent achievements of the company you are negotiating with, for instance. With this information, you'll be able to include details in your narrative that emphasize how your suggestion can assist them in reaching their particular objectives.

Be Real

When it comes to storytelling, authenticity is crucial. Credibility and trust are increased when sincere stories are shared, whether they are firsthand accounts or actual client endorsements. The other person is more likely to be convinced by your argument if they believe your story to be authentic. Genuine tales have a greater emotional impact and make a lasting impression, which increases the negotiation's overall impact.

Structure Your Story

A good story usually follows a well-defined format, with a beginning that establishes the scene, a middle that poses a problem or conflict, and a conclusion that resolves the issue and emphasizes the advantages. This format guarantees that your message is understood and helps keep attention. For example, begin with a situation or challenge that is relatable, then outline the difficulties encountered and end with a solution that highlights the advantages of your suggestion. A coherent narrative maintains the audience's interest while emphasizing the main points of your discussion.

Employ Vivid Details

Use descriptive language and vivid details to captivate your audience. This makes your story more captivating and memorable by helping them visualize it. Details make the story more relatable and realistic. . Say, for instance, "Our product reduced processing time by 30%, allowing the team to focus on more strategic tasks," rather than "Our product increased efficiency." These specifics give your argument tangible proof, which strengthens its persuasiveness.

Establish an Emotional Bond

Try to establish an emotional bond with your audience. To arouse empathy and strengthen your case, emphasize the human aspect of your tale. Decision-making is heavily influenced by emotions, and a story that arouses the appropriate feelings can have a big impact on how a negotiation turns out. Tell a tale, for instance, of how your solution turned around a failing company, emphasizing the individual experiences of those involved. This strategy not only demonstrates the useful advantages but also emotionally engages the audience, strengthening the persuasiveness of your proposal.

Using Social Proof and Authority

Strong persuasion techniques like social proof and authority rely on people's propensity to adopt the behaviors and viewpoints of others, particularly those they consider to be authorities or significant figures.

The idea that people are more likely to adopt a behavior if they observe others doing it is known as social proof. There are several ways to take advantage of this phenomenon, including displaying user-generated content, case studies, customer reviews, and testimonials. Potential clients are more inclined to trust and select your offering when they see that people just like them have had good experiences with it.

Conversely, authority appeals to people's regard for knowledge and reliability. You can influence people more successfully if you position yourself or your brand as an authority in your industry. Certifications, industry expert endorsements, media attention, and showcasing your knowledge and experience through webinars, whitepapers, and blog posts are all ways to build authority.

Take into account the following advice to optimize the influence of authority and social proof in your persuasion efforts:

Emphasize Positive Comments

Make sure your website and marketing materials prominently feature positive reviews, ratings, and testimonials. Positive testimonials from pleased clients are a potent form of social proof that reassures prospective customers about the caliber and dependability of your offering. To create a strong collection of social proof, ask your customers to share their experiences and write reviews.

Utilize Experts and Influencers

Work together with industry experts and influencers to promote your goods and services. Experts and influencers have built a devoted fan base and credibility, which makes their recommendations very convincing. Collaborate with them to produce genuine content that highlights the advantages and worth of your product.

Highlight Your Accomplishments and Milestones.

 To establish credibility, highlight your brand's achievements, including accolades, accreditations, and media appearances.

Emphasizing your accomplishments shows that you are an authority in your field. Industry honors, press attention, successful case studies, and any noteworthy accomplishments that distinguish you from rivals can all be examples of this.

Be Open and Truthful

 Make sure your assertions of authority and social proof are authentic and substantiated. Being genuine is essential to preserving trust. Steer clear of inflating or making up testimonials and endorsements as this can backfire and harm your reputation. Rather, concentrate on giving truthful and open information that demonstrates your credibility and authority.

Chapter 6

Overcoming Objections

Identifying Common Objections

It's not always as simple as calling a potential customer, making a pitch, and closing the deal to win a sale. Picky prospects will inevitably ask a lot of questions, voice complicated concerns, or, worse, refuse.

To handle such challenging sales calls and increase closed deals, objection handling is a fantastic strategy.

Breaking down the barriers your prospects put up during a sales call is the practice of objection handling, to put it simply.

You can persuade more people and increase your sales by being ready to address objections and allay any worries.

To find out how to address the most typical sales objections, continue reading.
How to deal expertly with sales objections
If you know how to properly address customer objections, you can use them to your advantage.

To help you become more adept at handling objections, consider the following best practices:
Pay close attention and try to understand your prospect.
Make your prospects feel valued by patiently listening to them.
During your sales call, demonstrating empathy will enable you to recognize the prospect's worries and provide you with the assurance to address any queries or worries while keeping the prospect's needs in mind.
Plan your response by posing follow-up questions. Prior to responding, a sales representative can ask pertinent follow-up questions to gain more

information about the prospect by cultivatingsituational awareness.

To get more information, it's best to leave these questions open-ended.

For each objection, develop a customized solution. There is no one-size-fits-all approach to addressing grievances. Every lead will have unique problems that you should try to solve with a solution that is specifically designed to meet their needs.

Create a guide on handling objections.

Keeping a record of every objection you encounter can be quite helpful. During your sales calls, prepare a possible answer or a series of follow-up questions for every kind of objection.

Techniques for Turning "No" to "Yes"

Has there ever been a difficult sales objection where you felt like you hit a brick wall? Imagining becoming an expert at sales negotiation and converting every "no" into a "yes" The majority of salespeople fear objections because they think they will put a stop to the discussion. .

However, what if objections are really opportunities waiting to be discovered?

We'll go over the two primary objection types that you'll face in business-to-business (B2B) sales as well as how to respond to the most prevalent ones. Are you prepared to change those "no's" to "yes's"? Let's get started.

Playing strategic chess is similar to navigating objections.

There are two primary routes for you. Recognize the objection and continue the conversation if it isn't important. The buyer's initial hesitancy usually goes away as they learn more about your product. If a small matter comes up, for instance, you can say, "Let's circle back to that," and carry on the discussion while emphasizing the advantages of your product.

Address the objection head-on if it's important. Ask questions to learn about their presumptions and emphasize the value of your service, for example, if budgetary concerns come up. When a potential customer says, "I just don't have the budget," you can answer, "Do you know what the price is?" and go over the cost-benefit analysis.

Let's now examine typical objections and how to respond to them.

"Now isn't a good time," a buyer may say, indicating that they haven't yet recognized the value. Explain the opportunity cost of inaction with compassion. "What would happen if you didn't solve this problem now?" is a question you may have.

"You're too expensive." is another typical objection. What matters is the perceived value, not the cost. Emphasize the advantages and return on investment to support the expense. Give instances of how your product has benefited people and the results they have observed.

Recall that you are in charge of the message. Although timing is difficult, the buyer's choice may be influenced by highlighting the opportunity cost of remaining unchanged. To overcome objections and convert hesitancies into commitments, employ these techniques.

Maintaining control without being Overbearing

Maintaining control of the conversation without being intrusive is essential to persuasion. The goal is to guide the conversation and deftly address objections without coming across as aggressive or controlling. Maintaining this equilibrium is crucial to fostering a courteous and fruitful dialogue.

To begin, practice active listening. Pay close attention to what your customer has to say and demonstrate your genuine concern for their problems. By summarizing and paraphrasing their thoughts, you can demonstrate that you genuinely comprehend their viewpoint.

It's critical to remain calm and patient despite resistance or skepticism. Respond to objections calmly and thoughtfully rather than becoming defensive or starting a fight.

Before responding to their concerns with answers or rebuttals, get their consent. They are more open to your recommendations, which demonstrates that you respect their opinion. You could ask, "Would it be okay if I shared some insights that might help clarify your concern?"

Presentations of options can also be highly effective. You empower your client and increase their receptivity to your suggestion by offering multiple solutions to the objection. You may respond, "We have a range of payment plans that could better suit your budget."

Building a relationship involves more than just finishing a transaction. Demonstrate your genuine concern for their needs and your dedication to identifying the best solution for them.
Using affirmative language is also essential. Your responses should be framed positively rather than negatively. Instead of replying, "You're wrong about our product," try saying, "I understand why you might think that, and here's some additional information that could be helpful."

After objections have been addressed, follow up to ensure the client has all the information they require and is satisfied with their choice. This builds your credibility and demonstrates your dedication to ensuring their satisfaction.

Chapter 7

Collaboration Negotiation Strategies

Building Long-Term Relationships

Building enduring relationships with clients and partners is another benefit of having strong negotiating skills. You can increase your value and reputation, build trust and respect, and produce win-win outcomes by using some effective negotiation techniques. This book will provide some advice on how to improve your professional relationships through the use of negotiation skills.

Recognize their interests and needs

Research the needs, interests, objectives, and difficulties of the other party before engaging in a negotiation. This will enable you to determine their goals, driving forces, and areas of discomfort so that you can modify your proposal appropriately. You can establish rapport and credibility while averting needless disputes or misunderstandings by demonstrating that you comprehend their viewpoint and sympathize with their circumstances.

Talk politely and clearly

For any negotiation or relationship to be successful, communication is essential. In addition to listening intently and politely to the opinions and concerns of the other person, you must also clearly and confidently express your own needs and interests. You must speak positively and constructively and refrain from using defensive or combative language. Open-ended questions, clarification of any presumptions or ambiguities, and a summary of the key points of agreement or disagreement are also necessary.

Look for value and reciprocal advantages

A successful negotiation is not a one-sided contest in which one side wins and the other loses. Instead, it is a cooperative process in which both sides aim to generate value and advantages for themselves. You must seek out areas of agreement, shared objectives, and innovative solutions that can meet the needs of both parties. Additionally, you must be adaptable and prepared to make compromises or trade-offs—as long as they are reasonable and well-balanced. By emphasizing value and benefits for both parties, you can improve your relationship and reputation while opening up new avenues for future collaboration.

Control your expectations and feelings
When there are complicated issues, competing interests, or high stakes involved, negotiating can be an emotionally taxing and stressful process. To keep your relationship healthy and fruitful, you must control both your own and the other person's feelings and expectations. You must use cool, collected arguments rather than emotional responses like rage, frustration, or resentment. Setting reasonable and attainable goals is also essential, as is avoiding making unfulfilled or excessive promises.

Observe and carry out
After the contract is finalized or the deal is signed, the negotiation continues. In addition to making sure the other party fulfills their end of the bargain,

you must follow up and fulfill your responsibilities. Reviewing the negotiation's results and outcomes is necessary, as is offering praise and comments. Additionally, you must stay in touch and communicate frequently, as well as handle any problems or worries that may come up. You can show your professionalism and dependability and increase your loyalty and trust by following up and carrying out your commitment.

Techniques for Creating Mutually Beneficial Outcomes

A mutually beneficial agreement, according to some negotiation experts, is one in which both parties take as much as they can from a limited supply of resources and call it a day.
We at the Program on Negotiation encourage you to set higher goals by fusing this kind of collaborative value creation with competitive value-claiming. It has been demonstrated to be the most effective way to reach a genuinely

advantageous agreement, not because it is the "nice" thing to do.

Because they approach negotiations with a win-lose mentality, negotiators frequently fall short of reaching a mutually beneficial agreement. It is true that negotiators are forced to bargain over a single issue in a limited number of agreements and disagreements, and that issue is typically price. For instance, you might find it difficult to broaden the discussion and bring up other topics when negotiating the cost of a rug at a foreign bazaar.

However, price is just one of many issues that are discussed in the great majority of business negotiations. For instance, you and your counterparty may discuss delivery, service, financing, potential future business deals, performance bonuses, and other topics in addition to price when negotiating a purchase agreement. Avoid the error of considering such complexity to be a drawback. The reverse is actually true. You can come up with trade-offs that both parties can agree on when there are several issues on the negotiation table.

You can accomplish more by making trade-offs than you would have if you had just made concessions on every issue. You improve your chances of coming to a win-win solution in the process.

Assume, for instance, that you place a high value on obtaining a solid service contract from your possible supplier. If you don't care as much about the financing terms, you could offer the supplier the financing terms they prefer and request a stronger service contract. You should have a bigger pie to split than when you began, but you can still work hard to assert value on each issue.

What are the real-world examples of this kind of value creation? Here are some examples to consider:

Following years of deadlock, the management of the Lincoln Center for the Performing Arts in New York City came to an agreement in 2014 to pay $15 million to Fisher's descendants in order to reclaim the lucrative naming rights to Avery Fisher Hall, which is home to the New York Philharmonic. Only after Lincoln Center management recognized and addressed the family's primary concern—that a planned renovation of the hall aligned with the objectives of their late patriarch—was a mutually beneficial agreement reached.

Mark Zuckerberg, the CEO of Facebook, convinced Kevin Systrom, the creator of Instagram, to sell his photo-sharing app for $1 billion in 2012. Following a series of cordial meetings where the two business titans discussed their respective business philosophies and, most importantly, Systrom disclosed how important he thought it was to keep Instagram separate from Facebook, the deal was finalized.

The Finnish mobile phone company Nokia was acquired by Microsoft in 2013 following months of unsuccessful negotiations. Only after Nokia set terms for the negotiations, such as that Microsoft provide Nokia with a source of funding, did a breakthrough occur.

What you should do right?

1. Exchange data

Negotiators frequently worry that by expressing their genuine preferences on a variety of topics, they will reveal too much. However, voicing preferences does not equate to revealing your financial situation. You could tell a prospective supplier, "That issue is critical to us, as our last supplier burned us with poor service." "What are your main concerns?"

2. Pose inquiries

Avoid the common blunder of considering negotiation as essentially an effort to influence the other party to comply with your wishes. You won't pay enough attention to what your counterpart has to say if you have that mindset because you will be too preoccupied with your talking points. On the other hand, you can gather the data you need to create a win-win agreement by actively listening and asking lots of questions.

3. **Present several comparable offers at the same time.**

One offer at a time is the norm for business negotiators. They gain very little new knowledge that would enable them to proceed if the offer is turned down. Making three offers that are distinct from one another but equally appealing to you is a better strategy. Even if the other party declines all three offers, she will probably let you know which one she prefers, which will help you move forward toward a win-win solution.

How to stay flexible without compromising Value

It can be difficult to strike a balance between being adaptable and not sacrificing value when negotiating. Consider it akin to walking a tightrope: you must remain loyal to your basic principles and objectives while simultaneously adjusting and adapting. To do that, follow these steps:

Recognize Your Basic Values

You must first be absolutely clear about the value that you contribute. This entails being intimately familiar with your offering and being aware of the precise ways in which it helps the other party. Determine the strengths and distinctive selling features that make you stand out from the competition. During negotiations, this information serves as your compass, keeping you from getting off course.

Establish definite boundaries

Establish your boundaries before engaging in any negotiations. Recognize what is non-negotiable and what your minimum acceptable terms are. This assists you in avoiding compromises that might diminish your worth. You know how far you can go without slipping off the tightrope, so it's similar to having a safety net.

Actively Listen

Understanding the needs and limitations of the other party is the first step towards being flexible. Pay attention to their goals and concerns. Listening intently to what they have to say is more important than simply waiting for your turn to speak. You can more easily spot areas where you can be accommodating without sacrificing your core principles if you have a better understanding of their viewpoint. For instance, rather than lowering the price, you might be able to provide flexible payment terms if cost is a barrier for them.

Seek out win-win situations

Try to find solutions that give each party a sense of accomplishment. This frequently entails thinking creatively and unconventionally to satisfy both sets of needs. Being flexible means coming up with alternatives that are still valuable, not caving in. For example, if a customer is unable to pay for your entire package, you might be able to provide a streamlined version that still offers the necessary advantages.

Remain Amenable to Compromise

Being adaptable entails being willing to make concessions, but doing so wisely is crucial. Set the things that are most important to you first, and be prepared to compromise on less important things. This demonstrates your willingness to cooperate with the other party while preserving the overall value proposition. Just make sure that any compromise doesn't make your offer seem less valuable.

Be Clear in Your Communication
The secret to successful negotiations is clear communication. Make sure the other person understands the value you're offering and make sure you communicate your points clearly and concisely. Be open and honest about your limitations and the reasons why some requests might not be possible. This openness fosters trust and makes it easier for the other person to appreciate your flexibility.

Have patience and perseverance.
Since negotiations can take some time, it's critical to maintain your composure and perseverance. Don't agree right away in order to get the deal done. Rather, spend some time considering all of your options and making sure that the final contract accurately represents the value you provide.

Being persistent can reassure the other party by demonstrating your dedication to coming up with a win-win solution.

Make Use of Objective Standards

Use objective standards whenever you can to bolster your argument. These could be particular performance metrics, market data, or industry benchmarks. Objective standards give your arguments a strong basis and support your position. Additionally, they assist in removing emotion from the negotiation process, which facilitates maintaining flexibility without sacrificing value.

Be Prepared to Leave

Being prepared to leave if the terms don't fit your objectives is sometimes the best way to preserve value. Knowing your value and refusing to settle for less is what this is all about, not being inflexible. Walking away guarantees that you don't compromise on your basic principles and frequently brings the other party back to the table with a better offer.

Think and Gain Knowledge

After every negotiation, consider what went well and what didn't. Gain knowledge from every encounter to strengthen your negotiating abilities. Adaptability is the foundation of flexibility, and the more you learn, the more adept you will be at preserving your position in future discussions.

You can maintain your flexibility during negotiations without sacrificing value by combining these tactics. It all comes down to being organized, comprehending the needs of both parties, and coming up with innovative ways to meet those needs without compromising your values.

Chapter 8

Navigating Complex Negotiations

Multiparty Negotiations

Multiparty negotiation is essentially any negotiation process in which three or more parties representing different interests take part. Three parties in a negotiation does not always indicate that it is multiparty, especially if two parties are negotiating for the same business or for the same objective. To meet the requirements for multiparty negotiation, three or more people promoting different points of view must be present.

To help you understand the concept, there are some basic similarities between two-party and multiparty negotiations. The similarities are as follows:

- Values must be found.
- The objective of creating value
- Solving problems together is crucial.
- How important it is to identify and clarify the interests of each party

In multi-party negotiations, these few similarities are just as crucial as in two-party ones.

Features That Set Multiparty Bargaining Apart
There are several clear differences between two-party and multiparty negotiations. These differences include many of the new skills you can learn by mastering the former.
The following are some crucial elements of a multiparty negotiation:

All parties have to work much harder outside of the negotiations. Research and strategy development will need to take place outside of the negotiation room.
The interactions during the negotiations are more intricate and multidimensional because there are more parties and variables involved.

The potential for some parties to draft agreements that exclude other parties if doing so would benefit them.

External elements like a company's political stance, values, etc. are becoming more and more significant.
Roles are frequently confused &more room for compromise.
More people can contribute more knowledge and creativity to the conversation.
This is a quick summary of some of the ways that multiparty negotiation varies from two-party negotiations. It's important to keep these changes in mind as you continue to experiment with the multiparty format.

Stages of a Multiparty Conversation
There are three phases to multiparty negotiation. By fully comprehending these phases, you can anticipate possible results and forecast the course of the process.

Before the Negotiation

During the pre-negotiation stage, the group decides who will take part in the negotiations. Parties typically specify their roles at this point Groups may also unite to form coalitions during this time. Setting clear objectives, needs, and boundaries before the negotiation is essential. Your ZOPA (zone of possible agreement) and BATNA (best alternative to a negotiated agreement) determine how well you can negotiate, especially when dealing with multiple parties. Having this information at your fingertips will help you make well-informed decisions during the negotiations. At the beginning of negotiations, it's also a good idea to share your ZOPA and pay attention to the other parties' boundaries. You can guide the discussion and steer clear of options that are outside of other parties' ZOPA by doing this.

Official Bargaining
The real negotiation begins at this stage. It is typically crucial to have a moderator in place for multiparty negotiations in order to help steer the discussion and ensure that all opinions are heard. It is easy for certain groups to dominate the

conversation and for others to be ignored when there is no moderator or chairman present. During multiparty negotiations, the moderator should set an agenda to keep the process moving in the right direction. Surveys, breakout brainstorming sessions, and other methods can help you come up with potential solutions.

Finally, it is crucial that the moderator has confidence in their ability to settle disputes because there will inevitably be disagreements and conflicts when there are a lot of different points of view. The moderator may need to remind disputing parties of the decorum and deference expected during negotiations. Respect for one another should always be maintained, even in the face of intense emotions.

Resolution or Concurrence

Following the discussions, the group can choose a plan of action, a solution, or a contract that works for the situation. An action plan and an implementation strategy are essential components of the solution since they serve as a roadmap for subsequent actions. If these issues have not been discussed, it may be difficult to put the changes that the groups agreed upon during negotiations into practice.

Dealing with Power Imbalances

It can be difficult to negotiate when there is an imbalance of power. Nonetheless, you can guarantee a fair result and level the playing field with the appropriate tactics. Here's how:

Recognize the Power Dynamics

First, it's important to understand the power dynamics at work. Authority, knowledge, resource control, confidence, and charisma are just a few of the many variables that can contribute to power. Finding the source of the power disparity will help you better plan your strategy.

Boost Your Self-Belief and Readiness
Power comes from knowledge.
You can negotiate with greater assurance if you are well-prepared. This entails doing in-depth research on the other party, comprehending their

requirements, and being aware of your own advantages and disadvantages. Clearly define your goals and options (also referred to as the Best Alternative to a Negotiated Agreement, or **BATNA**). Being prepared enables you to make well-informed decisions and maintain your composure in the face of pressure from the other party.

Put Relationship Building First
Power disparities can be lessened by fostering a positive relationship with the other party. If there is a sense of mutual respect or connection, people are more inclined to compromise. Engage in small talk at the beginning of the negotiation, demonstrate a sincere interest in the viewpoint of the other party, and work to establish a cooperative rather than hostile relationship. Recall that human connection is just as important in negotiations as the terms being discussed.

Look for Common Ground
Seek out objectives or common interests that both sides can support. You can change the emphasis from a power struggle to a cooperative approach to problem-solving by finding common ground.

This can assist in changing the negotiation's focus from a conflict of wills to one of cooperation toward a shared goal.

Apply objective standards.

Use objective benchmarks or standards whenever you can to bolster your claims. These could be industry norms, market data, or regulatory requirements. A neutral foundation offered by objective criteria can aid in the defusing of power dynamics. They make it more difficult for the more powerful side to ignore your arguments without coming across as irrational.

Pose Strategic Questions

You can learn more about the other person's priorities and limitations by posing open-ended questions. "What are your main concerns?" is one example. and "How can we make this work for both of us?" can help you identify leverage points and promote conversation. Additionally, asking questions demonstrates your interest and consideration, which can win you respect.

Control Your Feelings

Negotiations can be emotionally draining, particularly when there are power disparities. Even if the other person tries to threaten or control you, it's crucial to maintain your composure. Control your emotions and avoid letting annoyance or rage impair your judgment.
You can stay focused by using strategies like deep breathing, taking breaks, or even imagining successful outcomes.

Be Prepared to Leave

Being prepared to leave is one of the best negotiating stances. This does not imply that you should be combative, but rather that you are aware of your minimal acceptable terms and are ready to walk away if they are not fulfilled. Being aware of your best alternative to a negotiated agreement, or BATNA, offers you leverage and self-assurance. Additionally, it lets the other party know that you won't take an unfair bargain.

Look for Support and Allies

Bring in supporters or allies who can help maintain a balance of power if at all possible. These could be coworkers, professionals, or even legal advisors. Having more voices can help you resist excessive pressure and give your position more legitimacy.

Remain patient and persistent

When there is a power imbalance, the other party usually expects you to give in easily. Remain patient and persistent. The balance of power can occasionally be shifted just by refusing to give up right away. The other person may take your position more seriously if you are persistent in demonstrating your commitment and seriousness.

Think and Gain Knowledge

After every negotiation, consider what worked and what could be done better. Examine the power relationships and your approach to them. You can better prepare for upcoming negotiations and keep refining your negotiating techniques with this reflection.

Negotiating in High-stakes scenarios

Planning, strategy, and psychological awareness are all necessary for successful negotiation in high-stakes scenarios. These circumstances can be particularly frightening due to the grave repercussions involved, but if you approach them correctly, you can overcome them.

Preparation is essential.

High-stakes negotiations necessitate meticulous preparation. This means understanding all aspects of the negotiation, including the other party's needs, goals, and constraints. Analyze the background, interests, and negotiating style of the opposing side. Recognize your own objectives, constraints, and choices. Another part of preparation is gathering data, case studies, and any other relevant information that can support your position. Being well-prepared increases confidence and reduces the chance of being caught off guard.

Establish Clear Objectives

Decide on clear and specific goals for the negotiation. What are your non-negotiables and what do you hope to accomplish? Being aware of your goals keeps you on track and prevents you from making needless compromises. Establish attainable goals that take into account everyone's interests. Set priorities for your goals so you can decide what you must stick to and what you're willing to compromise on.

Establish rapport and trust

In high-stakes negotiations, establishing a rapport with the other party is essential. Building rapport and trust can improve communication and foster a more cooperative environment. Start by identifying areas of agreement or shared passion. Be genuinely interested in the needs and viewpoints of the other person. Be open and honest about your intentions while displaying empathy and respect. Reliability and constant, truthful communication are the keys to building trust.

Make Use of Strategic Framing

The negotiation can be greatly impacted by the way you frame your proposals and present the facts. When framing your offers and counteroffers, use language that is constructive and positive. Emphasize the advantages and worth that the other party will receive from your proposal. Keep the negotiation from being framed as a win-lose situation. Instead, concentrate on identifying win-win solutions. Proper framing can increase the appeal and acceptability of your proposals.

Regulate the Tempo

Controlling the negotiation's tempo is crucial. Avoid making snap decisions or rushing through conversations. Spend some time listening, thinking, and reacting. Ask clarifying questions or ask for more time to think over their proposals if the other party is trying to rush you into making a decision. Keeping the tempo under control allows you to remain calm and make wise choices.

Utilize Your BATNA

Your best alternative to a negotiated agreement, or BATNA, is your fallback option if the negotiation doesn't work out. You have more confidence and negotiating power when you know your BATNA. Additionally, it helps you set reasonable boundaries and avoid agreeing to unfavorable terms. If the other party thinks you have a strong BATNA, they may be more inclined to make a compromise.

Put interests ahead of positions

During high-stakes negotiations, it is important to focus on both parties' needs and underlying interests rather than just their stated positions. Positions are the specific demands or outcomes that each party wants, while interests are the reasons behind a party's stance. By understanding their interests, you can identify potential areas of agreement and create solutions that satisfy both sides. This tactic promotes collaboration and increases the likelihood of reaching a mutually beneficial agreement.

Use Silence as a Tool

Silence can be a very powerful tool in negotiations. If you pause before responding to an offer or statement, the other person may feel uneasy and be more inclined to make compromises or provide more details. Silence also gives you time to collect your thoughts and get ready to respond. Use it wisely to demonstrate that you are considering the proposal carefully and to leave room for introspection.

Be Ready to Make Changes

Flexibility is crucial in high-stakes negotiations. As the negotiation goes on, be prepared to adjust your strategies and tactics. Keep an open mind and be adaptable enough to change your plans as needed. Being flexible demonstrates your willingness to collaborate with others and develop creative solutions, which could be appealing to the other party.

Regulate Your Emotions

High-stakes negotiations can be emotionally draining, but it's important to remain calm. Having emotional control allows you to think clearly and make rational decisions. Avoid reacting hastily to provocations or pressure tactics. Make use of techniques for reducing stress and maintaining focus, such as mindfulness, deep breathing, and taking breaks.

Close with confidence.

When it comes time to finalize the agreement, have faith. Read the terms carefully to ensure that all of the agreement's details are understood and accepted.

Chapter 9

Negotiating in a Digital Era

Virtual Negotiation Best Practices

Developing virtual negotiation skills has become increasingly important in our post-2020 world. With globalization and remote work becoming more prevalent, procurement teams and sales professionals need to be able to negotiate effectively in virtual environments.

Virtual negotiation skills can sometimes be essential when working with remote teams, negotiating purchasing terms via video conferencing, or concluding international business transactions.

The Workings of Internet Bargaining

Virtual environments change the dynamics of negotiations; let's look at their quirks, challenges, and effective negotiating techniques.

Instead of shaking hands across a table, picture nodding your head at a pixelated screen. Many of the subtle cues that people use to convey their thoughts through body language are no longer present, and you have a new set of rules to follow.

Best practices to ensure positive outcomes in virtual settings:

Be Well Prepared

Just like in-person negotiations, prep is key. After learning about the other party's needs and interests, you should prepare your own goals and options. Make sure your internet connection is dependable, and familiarize yourself with the virtual platform you intend to use. Make sure you have all the information you require on hand, and prepare documents and presentations in advance. Because technical problems can disrupt the flow, always have a backup plan, like a phone call, in case the technology fails.

Select the Right Platform

Choose a trustworthy online meeting platform that offers necessary features such as screen sharing, breakout areas, and recording capabilities. Ensure that the platform is comfortable for all users. Popular choices include Google Meet, Microsoft Teams, and Zoom; each has unique features that can help you negotiate more effectively. To efficiently set up meetings and avoid time zone conflicts, use scheduling tools.

Clearly define objectives and agendas

Ensure that everyone is aware of the objectives and agenda before the meeting. This keeps the discussion on topic and ensures that everyone is in agreement. An agenda allows participants to prepare their questions and ideas in advance and provides a roadmap for the conversation. Give each item on the agenda enough time to be discussed in order to conduct the meeting efficiently.

Establish ground rules for the virtual negotiation to maintain a professional and courteous environment.

This includes guidelines for speaking, muting microphones, and utilizing chat features. Ground rules contribute to a well-structured and orderly meeting by preventing interruptions and ensuring that everyone has an opportunity to contribute. Encourage participants to use the "raise hand" feature when they want to speak in order to avoid interrupting one another.

Establish a Professional Environment

Select a peaceful, well-lit area for the discussion. Make sure your background is professional and clear. .Dress as if you were going to a face-to-face meeting. Keeping your workspace tidy and free of clutter demonstrates your professionalism and appreciation for the negotiating process. Consider using a neutral virtual background if your physical surroundings aren't the best.

Be Active

Be proactive throughout the negotiation. Make eye contact by looking straight into the camera, talk concisely and clearly, and be aware of your body language. Encourage everyone to participate and make sure they all have a chance to speak. By addressing each person by name, you build rapport and make the conversation more personal. Distribute the notes you took during the meeting to ensure that everyone is aware of the key decisions and points.

Use Visual Aids

Make use of charts, graphs, and slides to support your points. Visual aids can help explain complex ideas and keep the audience interested. By adding interactive elements like surveys and Q&A sessions, the virtual negotiation can become more lively and interactive. Give out documents in advance so that participants have time to review them before the meeting.

Be Aware of Time Zones

If participants are in different time zones, schedule the meeting at a time that is convenient for all. When making plans, consider time differences. Use tools like World Time Buddy or Google Calendar's time zone feature to find the ideal times for meetings. When scheduling, consider cultural and regional holidays as they may impact availability.

Follow Up

After the virtual negotiation, give a summary of the discussion, the issues that were resolved, and the next steps. This ensures clarity and keeps things moving forward. Send a comprehensive email or formal document outlining the key findings and next steps. Arrange follow-up meetings if necessary to go over any outstanding concerns and track developments.

Using Technology And Tools to Your Advantage

Any professional who wishes to get the best results for their projects, clients, and organizations must be able to negotiate contracts. Contract negotiations can be difficult, time-consuming, and stressful, though, particularly when handling complicated, multi-party, or cross-cultural situations. Thankfully, technology can help you become a better contract negotiator by giving you the tools, resources, and insights you need to improve your teamwork, communication, and preparation. We'll look at six ways in which you can use technology to strengthen your contract negotiation abilities .

Make use of online resources

One advantage of technology is that it gives you access to online resources that can make contract negotiations easier and more efficient. For instance, you can save time, money, and paper by using platforms that let you draft, send, sign, and manage contracts electronically. In order to draft and review contracts more quickly and effectively, you can also use platforms that provide templates, clauses, and best practices for various contract types. In order to negotiate remotely and safely, you can also make use of platforms that allow online communication and collaboration with your counterparts, like chat, video conferencing, and file sharing.

Utilize analytics and data

Utilizing data and analytics to enhance your contract negotiation abilities is another benefit of technology. To help you adjust your negotiating strategy and tactics, you can, for instance, use data and analytics to investigate and comprehend the needs, preferences, and behavior of your counterparts. In order to make well-informed and logical decisions, you can also use data and analytics to assess and contrast various contract options, scenarios, and results. Additionally, data and analytics can be used to track and evaluate contract performance, compliance, and satisfaction, which will assist you in locating and resolving any problems or disagreements.

Make use of AI

Using artificial intelligence (AI) to enhance your contract negotiation abilities is a third advantage of technology. Contract drafting, review, editing, and summarization are just a few of the repetitive, time-consuming, or complicated tasks that can be automated and optimized with AI.

AI can also be used to help and counsel you during the negotiating process. For example, it can offer you insights, comments, and recommendations based on your values, interests, and goals. Additionally, you can use AI to analyze your opportunities, weaknesses, and strengths in order to learn from and get better at contract negotiations.

Make use of simulation and gamification

A fourth benefit of technology is that it enables you to enhance your contract negotiation abilities through simulation and gamification. For instance, by playing games, scenarios, or challenges that replicate actual contract negotiation situations, you can use gamification and simulation to practice and improve your contract negotiation skills in an enjoyable, captivating, and interactive way. Additionally, you can test and improve your contract negotiation skills in a safe, regulated, and feedback-rich environment by using gamification and simulation. For example, you can receive feedback, rewards, or scores based on your performance, actions, or results.

Make use of networking and social media

The ability to use social media and networking to strengthen your contract negotiation abilities is the fifth advantage of technology. For instance, social media and networking can be used to create and preserve connections with stakeholders, influencers, and counterparts, which will help you build credibility, rapport, and trust. Additionally, social media and networking can be used to exchange knowledge and learn from mentors, experts, and other contract negotiation professionals. Additionally, by showcasing and promoting your accomplishments, value, and contract negotiation skills on social media and networking, you can draw in and hold on to more opportunities, clients, and partners.

Make use of learning and personal growth
The sixth benefit of technology is that it enables you to enhance your contract negotiation abilities through learning and personal growth. For instance, by enrolling in online courses, tests, or coaching sessions, you can use personal development and learning to evaluate and enhance your knowledge,

abilities, and mindset in contract negotiations. Additionally, you can use learning and personal development to broaden and diversify your knowledge, abilities, and mindset in contract negotiations by investigating novel subjects, fashions, or viewpoints. Additionally, by using new tools, resources, or updates, you can use personal development and learning to update and refresh your knowledge, mindset, and contract negotiation skills.

Managing Remote Buyer Interactions

Building trust, sustaining engagement, and guaranteeing effective communication all depend on managing interactions with remote buyers. The following advice can help you handle these interactions:

By Building Rapport

In remote interactions, rapport-building is essential. Begin by identifying areas of agreement, demonstrating a sincere interest in the buyer's requirements, and acting in a cordial yet expert manner. A more laid-back atmosphere can be created and the ice broken with small talk.

Personalize Communication

To help the buyer feel appreciated and understood, personalize your communication. Make use of their name, bring up earlier discussions, and modify your messages to speak to their particular requirements and worries. Personalized correspondence demonstrates your concern for the buyer's particular circumstance.

Speak Clearly and Concisely

In remote interactions, it is crucial to communicate clearly and succinctly. Steer clear of jargon and speak simply. Make sure your messages are clear and concise by summarizing the important points. Charts and infographics are examples of visual aids that can improve the way complex information is communicated.

Use a Variety of Communication Channels

To maintain contact with customers, use a variety of communication channels. Instant messaging, video conferences, phone conversations, and emails can all fall under this category. Select the channel that best fits the buyer's preferences and the situation. Continual updates via various platforms can keep customers informed and interested.

Be Available and Responsive

Prompt responses show your dedication and dependability. Make an effort to answer buyer questions as soon as possible and be accessible for follow-up conversations. To foster trust, establish and follow response time expectations.

Make Use of Interactive and Visual Content.

 Use interactive and visual content to improve remote interactions. Distribute product demos, infographics, and presentations to effectively engage customers and make your points. Live polls and Q&A sessions are examples of interactive content that can enhance interaction and encourage participation.

Plan Frequent Check-Ins

Plan frequent check-ins to keep things moving forward and to answer any queries or worries. Consistent touchpoints aid in maintaining the buyer's interest and knowledge during the negotiating process. During these check-ins, give them updates, solicit their opinions, and reaffirm your dedication to their needs.

Collect and Respond to Input

Ask customers for feedback to learn about their experiences and pinpoint areas that need work. To demonstrate that you appreciate their opinions and are dedicated to ongoing development, take action on their suggestions. To get feedback and show that you are responsive, use surveys and follow-up emails.

Preserve Professionalism

Be extremely professional in all of your communications from a distance. This entails being on time, organized, and courteous. Being professional aids in gaining the buyer's confidence and trust.

Make sure that all written and verbal communications are courteous, professional, and unambiguous.

Adjusting to the Age of Digital

We now negotiate differently as a result of the digital age, which presents both opportunities and difficulties. You can successfully navigate the complexities of digital negotiations by embracing technology, honing your virtual communication skills, and keeping an eye on developing solid relationships. In this constantly changing environment, staying current with the newest tools and best practices will guarantee that you stay productive and competitive.

Chapter 10

Closing The Deal

Techniques for a Seamless Close

The process of closing a deal is delicate and calls for a combination of skill, intuition, and preparation. Clear communication and a deep comprehension of the client's needs must be established well in advance to guarantee a smooth close. Establishing trust is essential; the customer should have faith that the solution being provided is customized to meet their particular needs. Actively listening during the negotiating process guarantees that any issues or skepticism are resolved quickly, eliminating any opportunity for hesitation as the deal moves closer to completion.

Furthermore, a clear presentation of the agreement reduces misunderstandings and fosters an atmosphere of openness.

Refrain from giving the client too many details at the last minute, as this may raise unwarranted questions. Rather, provide a succinct but persuasive synopsis of the value proposition that restates the advantages they will experience. Since confidence spreads easily, closing the deal with clarity and zeal can frequently encourage the client to feel the same way.

Explain the Main Points

Start by providing a summary of the agreement's key points. This guarantees that there are no misunderstandings and that both parties are in agreement. Emphasize the advantages for both parties and the ways in which their interests have been taken into consideration.

Verify Agreement Details

Review the terms and conditions in detail once more. This covers terms of payment, due dates, obligations, and any unforeseen circumstances.

Instill a Sense of Urgency

Instill a sense of urgency in the other party to motivate them to take action. Instead of putting pressure on them, emphasize the benefits of closing the deal right away. Mention any limited-time offers or time-sensitive benefits that are included in the contract.

Use Positive Language

When talking about the close, use language that is upbeat and assured. Assume they are prepared to sign and frame your questions appropriately rather than asking if they are. For instance, "I'll prepare the final paperwork for us to sign," or "Let's go ahead and finalize this."

Proactively Address Issues

Foresee any lingering issues or objections and resolve them before they arise. This shows that you are paying attention and are prepared to make sure the closing goes well.

Confirm the Value

Remind the other party of the benefits and value of the agreement. Reiterating the value eases any residual uncertainty and helps them make a firm decision.

Make a Clear Call to Action

Clearly state what has to be done to complete the transaction. Make sure the other party is aware of exactly what to do when signing a contract, paying, or setting up a follow-up meeting.

Recognizing the Right Time to Seal the Agreement

When it comes to closing a deal, timing is crucial. It takes close observation and an acute understanding of the client's decision-making process to identify the ideal time. The client asking specific implementation questions, talking about timelines, or expressing enthusiasm for the outcomes your product or service can produce are all indications that the time is right.

However, it can backfire to rush into a close too soon. The client may hesitate or even withdraw if they feel pressured before they are ready. For this reason, it's important to pay attention to both verbal and nonverbal clues, such as a confident tone of voice or positive body language. It can be easier to seal the deal if you follow up on these cues with tactful but assured closing statements, like inquiring about the next steps or reaffirming their commitment.

When it comes to closing a deal, timing is crucial. Choosing the appropriate time to sign the contract can have a big impact:

Seek out buying signals.
Keep an eye out for nonverbal and verbal clues that suggest the other person is prepared to commit. These could be demonstrating enthusiasm for the agreement, nodding, agreeing to important points, or posing targeted implementation-related questions.

Assess Agreement
It's a good sign that the time is right if both parties have agreed on all significant points and there are no outstanding issues. You're closer to closing if the negotiating process has gone more smoothly.

Test the Waters
To determine preparedness, use trial closes. You can determine whether the other party is prepared to complete the transaction by using phrases like "How does that sound to you?" or "Are we ready to move forward?"

Avoid Over-Negotiating

Refrain from continuing to negotiate after you have come to a mutually agreeable conclusion. Excessive bargaining may cause new problems and even ruin the agreement.

Trust Your Instincts

Knowing when to close is largely dependent on experience and intuition. Have faith in your intuition and the clues you're getting from the other person.

Handling Last-Minute Pushbacks

Last-minute concerns or objections are normal and should be seen as a chance rather than a failure. Near the end, a client's hesitation or concern is frequently a sign of a need for assurance rather than a flat rejection. When these situations are handled professionally and empathetically, possible roadblocks can be transformed into moments of mutual trust.

Allow the client to fully express their concerns before calmly acknowledging the pushback. Whether it's about cost, implementation, or uncertainties about results, active listening demonstrates that their perspective is valued. Directly address the objection and respond with concise, fact-based arguments that support the worth and dependability of your solution. To allay their concerns, provide extra reassurances, like guarantees or follow-up assistance, or share success stories if needed.

Flexibility is also essential; occasionally, a small incentive or change to the terms can help advance the conversation without jeopardizing the integrity of the agreement. You can effectively close the deal and boost the client's confidence by using last-minute pushbacks as an opportunity to remain calm and solution-focused.

Remain Calm and Composed Retain your cool and refrain from expressing anger. Pushbacks at the last minute are frequent and can be handled coolly and collectedly and also pay attention to the issues or criticisms that are being voiced.

Sometimes all that is needed by the other party is confirmation or clarification on a specific issue. You can comprehend their viewpoint and respond to it effectively by listening to them.

Treat Issues Straightforwardly

Address the criticisms directly by giving succinct, understandable responses. To bolster your argument and allay any concerns, provide evidence in the form of statistics, testimonies, or prior agreements.

Reiterate the Benefits of the Agreement

Remind the other party of the advantages and worth of the transaction. This can assist in shifting the conversation back to the advantages and the original motivations for their interest.

Offer Alternatives

Provide compromises or other options if a specific term is making you hesitant. Being adaptable can help you get past objections and show that you're willing to work toward a solution.

Assure Openness

Be open and honest about your role and any limitations you may have. Being truthful fosters trust and demonstrates your dedication to a just and advantageous agreement.

Confirm Commitment

After the issues have been resolved, ask if they are still committed to proceeding. They can seal the deal and avoid more resistance by restating their commitment.

Document Changes

Be sure to thoroughly record any modifications made to the agreement as a result of the pushback. This guarantees that the final terms are understood by both parties.

Chapter 11

Evaluation Negotiation Outcomes

Measuring Success Beyond Numbers

It's simple to become obsessed with numbers during negotiations, whether they be the final numbers on a contract, the terms of the agreement, or the price. But genuine negotiation success extends beyond the monetary results. Some strategies for evaluating success that offer a more comprehensive perspective and produce good negotiation outcomes are listed below;

Developing Powerful Connections

The relationship that you establish with the other party is one of the most crucial elements of a successful negotiation.

Future opportunities, increased cooperation, and a favorable reputation in your sector can all result from a solid relationship. Even if the current transaction doesn't result in the biggest profit, a strong rapport can pave the way for future advantages. A successful outcome is largely dependent on the mutual respect, trust, and understanding that are developed during the negotiating process.

Reaching a State of Mutual Contentment
Both parties should be happy with the result of a successful negotiation. Both parties may feel their basic needs were met and respected, but this does not necessarily imply that they received everything they desired. The groundwork for a future cooperative and fruitful relationship is laid when both parties leave with a positive impression of the agreement.

Improving Credibility and Reputation

Your reputation both personally and professionally can be greatly impacted by the way you negotiate. During negotiations, you can increase your credibility and establish yourself as a preferred partner for future agreements by acting with honesty, equity, and respect. Achieving success involves more than just getting the deal right away; it also involves how you are viewed in the business world. Future opportunities and more amicable negotiations may result from having a reputation as a trustworthy and equitable negotiator.

Adding Value Outside of the Sale

Think about the benefits of a negotiation that go beyond the final agreement. This could entail learning more about the other party's industry, spotting untapped markets, or making contacts that might prove useful in the future. One important indicator of success is the capacity to add value, such as by looking into joint ventures or cooperative projects.

Providing Longevity and Sustainability

On paper, a deal may seem good, but it may not be sustainable over time. Agreements reached through successful negotiations are realistic, useful, and long-lasting. It is essential to make sure that the conditions of the agreement are enduring and enforceable by both sides. It's about establishing a win-win situation where both parties can observe the advantages of the agreement develop over time, resulting in ongoing cooperation and success.

Development on Both a Personal and Professional Level

Every negotiation serves as a teaching moment. Every negotiation offers chances for both professional and personal development, regardless of whether you win or lose. Throughout time, you can improve your negotiating skills by thinking back on what worked and what could be done better. Beyond the immediate transaction, the abilities you acquire—like active listening, empathy, strategic thinking, and problem-solving—are priceless and help you succeed overall.

Conflict Resolution and Emotional Intelligence

Controlling your own and the other party's emotions is essential to fruitful negotiations. Having high emotional intelligence makes it easier to handle difficult circumstances, comprehend underlying issues, and create a constructive negotiation atmosphere. Strong negotiating abilities are demonstrated by the ability to resolve disputes during negotiations, which can result in more satisfying and long-lasting agreements.

Adaptability and Flexibility

A crucial component of a successful negotiation is the capacity to adjust to shifting conditions and fresh information. Being adaptable does not entail sacrificing one's moral principles; rather, it means being receptive to different approaches and innovative approaches to problems. Being flexible can result in more creative and successful agreements by proving that you can manage dynamic and complicated negotiation situations.

After the Negotiation

Negotiation success continues after the contract is signed. Good follow-up guarantees that the agreement's conditions are carried out without hiccups and that any problems are resolved right away. By staying in touch and checking in with the other party, you demonstrate your dedication to the partnership and the agreement, which strengthens mutual respect and collaboration.

Long-Term Effects

Think about how the agreement will affect your personal or professional objectives in the long run. Success is about how the agreement fits into your larger strategy and goals, not just about short-term gains. A successful agreement is one that supports your strategic goals and is in line with your long-term vision.

Learning from Successes and Failures

Every negotiation encounter offers valuable insights and lessons, making learning from both successes and failures in the field akin to searching through a treasure trove of experiences. It is an ongoing process of growth, introspection, and discovery. When a negotiation ends well, it's critical to recognize the factors that led to that favorable result. It might have been the rapport you developed with the other person, or it might have been your careful planning and awareness of their requirements. In addition to celebrating the victory, it's important to analyze it and determine what factors contributed to its success. Consider the methods you employed, the mutual respect that was developed, and the effectiveness of your communication. These triumphs are more than just wins; they serve as models for further discussions.

Failures, on the other hand, can be difficult, but they are also opportunities for some of the most important learning. When a negotiation doesn't work out, it offers a unique perspective on your tactics and approach.

It may be painful at first, but stand back and consider what went wrong. Was there a lack of planning? Did you fail to notice important cues from the other person? Or perhaps you were overcome by your feelings? It's important to comprehend these elements. In order to improve future results, it's important to accept your mistakes without feeling bad about them.

Regular reflection on accomplishments and shortcomings is essential. Spend some time considering what went well and what didn't during each negotiation. Think about the decision-making process, the dynamics, and the communication styles. Did you listen intently and with compassion? Have you remained adaptive and flexible? Important insights may be gained from these reflections.

Asking for feedback is just as important as conducting introspection.. Ask for the viewpoint of the other person or your coworkers if appropriate.

They may draw your attention to things you missed or offer helpful criticism that can be very eye-opening. In addition to improving your learning process, this feedback loop allows you to view the negotiation from a variety of perspectives.

The key here is to always strive for improvement. Continue to be curious and to improve your abilities. Attend workshops, read up on negotiation strategies, and practice frequently. Regardless of the outcome, every negotiation broadens your experience base. You will become more skilled, more perceptive, and more self-assured over time. Therefore, have an open mind and a willingness to learn as you embrace both your accomplishments and your failures.

Your path to becoming a skilled negotiator includes every encounter and exchange. It's not just about closing the deal; it's about growing and changing with each step.

Implementing Feedback for Future Growth

Implementing feedback for future growth is a transformative process that can significantly enhance your effectiveness and negotiating skills. Here's a detailed approach to making the most of the feedback you receive:

Embrace a Growth Mindset

The first step in using feedback effectively is cultivating a growth mindset. This means viewing criticism as an opportunity to improve rather than as an assessment of your abilities. It involves understanding that skill development can result from diligence and hard work, and that feedback is a crucial instrument in this process.

Engage in Active Listening

When someone gives you feedback, listen intently and actively. Focus on understanding the criticism rather than immediately responding or defending your actions. This can be challenging, especially if the criticism is severe, but it's important to consider all of the information before responding.

Request Specific Remarks

General feedback is less helpful than specific feedback. Encourage those providing feedback to be detailed and specific. Ask questions to gain clarification and gain a better understanding of the issues being raised. Ask for concrete examples or suggestions on how to improve your communication, for example, instead of taking remarks like "You need to communicate better."

Think about the remarks.

Consider the feedback you have received. Consider how it aligns with your self-evaluation and experiences. By reflecting on the feedback, you can gain a deeper understanding of its root causes and how it contributes to your overall growth and development.

Look for Trends

Examine your feedback for any patterns or reoccurring themes. When multiple sources highlight the same issues, it's an obvious indication that these areas require attention. You can clearly see where to focus your efforts by looking at feedback patterns.

Set Achievable Goals

Transform criticism into specific, achievable goals. Break down the criticism into manageable assignments that you can finish. If the feedback is about improving your negotiating skills, for example, set goals like attending a negotiation workshop, practicing active listening, or role-playing negotiation scenarios.

Create a development plan.

Make a detailed plan that outlines the steps you will take to implement the suggestions. Include due dates, required materials, and milestones to track your progress. You stay accountable and focused when you have a well-organized plan.

Seek out assistance and resources.

Never be afraid to seek out tools and support to implement feedback. These could be books, training programs, mentorship, or online courses. By exposing you to new concepts and techniques, using these resources can aid in your personal development.

Utilize and Practice

The best way to implement feedback is to practice. Track your progress and apply the criticism in real-world situations. For example, at your next meeting, try being more assertive in negotiations if you've been told to do so. See how it goes.

Monitor Your Development

Regularly assess your progress toward your objectives. Think about what is working well and what needs further adjustment. By monitoring your progress, you can stay on track and make necessary adjustments to your development plan.

Continue to Be Open to Constant Feedback

Feedback is not a one-time event; it is a continuous process. Maintain your openness to criticism and use it to improve yourself. By regularly checking in with mentors, peers, or supervisors, you can stay on track with your development goals and get timely feedback.

Respect the Advancement

Along the way, acknowledge your achievements and progress. Recognizing your successes motivates you to keep working toward improvement and strengthens positive behavior. Telling a peer or mentor who is encouraging about your progress or just congratulating yourself on your achievements is the easiest way to celebrate.

Examine and Adjust

As you progress and put the advice into practice, keep reflecting on your past experiences and adjusting your approach as needed. Being adaptable ensures that you're always improving because personal development is an ongoing process.

Chapter 12

Maintaining The Relationship

Post Negotiation Follow-Up Strategies

Breaking the deal is just half the fight.

Hello, welcome to the fascinating world of post-negotiation follow-up. It's not just about closing the deal; it's also about keeping the relationship going. For example, let's say you've just negotiated a fantastic contract. The next step is straightforward communication. Maintain the conversation after the handshake. It's similar to caring for a freshly sewn plant; your efforts could mean the difference between a one-time transaction and a long-term collaboration.

A brief phone conversation, a quick email, or a simple thank-you note can make a big difference. Every deal is the start of a new relationship, and in the world of business, relationships are everything.

Therefore, make sure your post-negotiation follow-up is as strong as your negotiation game because it's not just about the money; it's about the people. Why just win the battle when you can win the war? That is why post-negotiation follow-up is so powerful.

Building Client Loyalty Through Trust and Value

It's similar to fostering a long-term relationship to cultivate client loyalty through negotiation value and trust. It takes more than just closing a deal to build a long-lasting foundation of respect and understanding.

Think of the first few rounds of negotiations as the start of a partnership. The cornerstones of trust are openness and truthfulness. Setting the stage for a deeper connection occurs when you approach negotiations with a sincere desire to comprehend and satisfy your clients' needs.

Active listening, empathy, and being honest about your strengths and weaknesses show that you value the relationship more than the transaction.

The next step is to create value.
Understanding your client's priorities and providing solutions that meet their unique needs are more important than simply making a good offer. This can entail going above and beyond to tailor your offer, offering advice that helps them make better choices, or continuing to be there for them even after the sale is finalized. Making your customers feel as though they are receiving more than they originally paid for is the essence of value.

Being consistent is essential to establishing trust. Clients start to view you as dependable and trustworthy when you deliver on your commitments, meet deadlines, and keep lines of communication open. Small acts taken over time are what establish a strong reputation.

Building trust takes time and a series of constructive encounters.

Expressing gratitude is an additional crucial element. Acknowledge the significance of your client's business. Small actions can have a significant impact, such as remembering their preferences, sending follow-up calls to inquire about their satisfaction, or writing thank-you notes. You can tell they are more than just a source of income by taking these steps.

Trust is also fostered by transparency during negotiations. By being clear about terms, prices, and any potential difficulties, you can avoid misunderstandings and establish your credibility. When customers believe they are getting the full picture, they value it and are more inclined to be honest in return.

Adaptability and responsiveness to client needs are also key components of fostering client loyalty. A client will have more faith in your capacity to adjust and assist them if they perceive that your understanding of their particular needs is recognized and provided with flexibility.

Changing the terms, coming up with different solutions, or being accessible to quickly address their concerns could all be part of this.

Client relationships can be further strengthened by thinking back on previous negotiations and getting input. Find out what worked and what needs improvement by asking your clients. This gives you insights to keep improving your strategy in addition to demonstrating that you respect their viewpoint.

Essentially, establishing client loyalty via value and trust is an ongoing process that involves engagement, openness, and providing outstanding value. It's about establishing a partnership where clients feel appreciated, understood, and supported, which fosters a devoted relationship that eventually works out well for both sides.

Turning Clients into Advocates

Every brand needs to understand the customer experience that accompanies relocating from one nation to another. The initial step is awareness, where you communicate your existence through authentic word-of-mouth or public relations, and the following step is consideration.

This step is crucial if you want your customers to evolve into brand advocates.

Transitioning them to the third step on your journey, this is where you showcase that you offer the best choices and deals. They will make purchases from your website's product page or physical store, but your efforts shouldn't end there. You need to deliver on your commitments by providing the product or service, while also ensuring their satisfaction through loyalty programs. It's important to stay connected with them because they've developed an affinity for your brand by now. I trust you enjoyed this journey. Create a community, a platform, and grant programs as these will empower them to promote your brand and discuss it.

CONCLUSION

As we conclude our exploration of the **Techniques for Sales Negotiation**, let's pause to consider the most important lessons learned, the ongoing development of your abilities, and some parting words of wisdom for your future.

Important Lessons for Successful Sales Negotiation
A dance of empathy, understanding, and human connection, negotiation is so much more than a set of tactics. Although preparation is your cornerstone, your success is greatly influenced by how you establish rapport, communicate clearly, and maintain flexibility. Building value and concentrating on win-win results prepares the ground for enduring, sustainable collaborations.

And it can make all the difference to close the deal with clarity, confidence, and a sincere sense of urgency.

The Ongoing Development of Negotiation Techniques

As a negotiator, your path is never static. Every encounter, every transaction, whether successful or not, teaches us something. Accept the criticism you get, look for new information, and be flexible at all times. The negotiation industry is always changing, particularly with the introduction of new digital tools and technologies. Maintain your curiosity, keep improving, and understand that every negotiation is a chance to develop and improve your strategy.

Concluding Remarks to Encourage Sales Professionals

You are a relationship builder, a problem solver, and a value creator in the sales industry, not just a negotiator. Keep in mind that every negotiation is an opportunity to benefit both your business and the people you are negotiating with.

Be transparent, empathetic, and genuinely interested in learning about and meeting the needs of the other person in every conversation.

You will stand out for your ability to handle the difficulties of negotiation with poise, tolerance, and perseverance. Instead of letting failures depress you, see them as priceless teaching moments that advance your mastery. Honor your accomplishments, take lessons from your mistakes, and never stop aiming for greatness.

William Ury, the legendary negotiator, once said, "Be soft on the person, hard on the problem in negotiation." Prioritize fostering relationships while resolutely tackling the current problems. The secret to attaining successful and long-lasting results is striking this balance.

Keep these tips in mind, and I hope your sales negotiating career is full of development, achievement, and enduring relationships. Continue to aim for greatness and never forget that every accomplishment is evidence of your perseverance and commitment. You're capable!

www.ingramcontent.com/pod-product-compliance
Lightning Source LLC
Chambersburg PA
CBHW071029240526
45469CB00006BD/2141